The Original THEBAN WORKBOOK

Printing History
First Edition - 2005
Second Edition -2015

Cover illustration by GoldenPhi Press

Theban Today is a Trademark.

Published by GoldenPhi Press, LLC (www.GoldenPhiPress.com)

GoldenPhi Press, LLC
Minnesota

ATTENTION: SCHOOLS AND CORPORATIONS

THEBAN TODAY[TM] books are available at quantity discounts with bulk purchase for educational, business, or sales promotional use. For information please email us directly at:
purchase-bulk@thebantoday.com

HOW TO CONTACT US
ERRORS: error-submission@thebantoday.com.
RECOMMENDATIONS: my-recommendation@thebantoday.com
COMMENTS, QUESTIONS, CONCERNS: inquiries@thebantoday.com

WEBSITE: www.ThebanToday.com

Contents

Author's Note

I myself wanted to learn the writings of this mystical and magickal THEBAN SCRIPT (pronounced thē-bann). Finding the teaching materials to learn was close to impossible. My goal was to read and write Theban fluently but no one had any tutorials available to help people like myself learn to read and write the Theban alphabet. There were references from books with different variations of the magickal alphabet to choose from, but they were limited on how to learn the script. If you may now know, there are several variations of the Theban alphabet. You now have the option to pick what is closest to your hearts in the way of writing any flavor of Theban.

By no means is this workbook a replacement to the Theban Alphabet that you have learned and used over the years. I have put together the information I have learned and wish to share with you. The type of Theban you will be learning is the modernized version that will work with common day letters like 'J', 'U' and 'W' which are not available in some Theban scripts. This workbook was created to help anyone who would like to learn to read and write Theban, no matter which variation they know, or choose from. Your magickal script that has been passed down from generation to generation will not be replaced with what you see in this workbook. You can completely ignore the characters used here, but you can still utilize some of the tools available to help pass your ancient writings onto your children. This workbook is special in a way that it can be used by all no matter what flavor of Theban you wish to learn.

To teach myself, I used the same format used in this book. Once I learned the THEBAN ALPHABET, I created several booklets like this one and passed them amongst strangers and friends to see what kind of feedback I would get. They found the workbook easy to use, very well organized, and amazed at how they can read and write Theban in a short period of time. "I wish something like this was available years ago" was the general consensus among the group. With such a positive response, I wanted to share it with all of you, hoping you'll find the same joy and experience as we did in having the ability to read and write Theban.

I hope you enjoy this workbook. A lot of hard work has gone into it. Peace to all!

- **Gealhain Samlach**

How to Use This Book

Start at the beginning of the workbook and learn at your own pace. With 27 characters to learn, you could set a goal to learn them all in 27 days or less – one character a day. You will learn the vowels first, then the rest of the letters. Learning the vowels first will give you a chance to form words while you're learning.

Navigational Strip: This is located at the top-center of the page of each new character you are about to learn. It will tell you what you are currently working on (the letter is underlined) and what you just learned (these letters are shown in Theban). The example below tells us that you are learning the letter 'O' and also shows the characters you have learned (A, E, and I).

B C D F G H J K L M N O P Q R S T U V W X Y Z .

Given Letter: This box is located on the left-hand side of the page and indicates which letter you are about to learn. The roman letter is shown below and just above it will be the Theban letter you will be learning.

How to Write the Character: Each new section will have an area to teach you how to write the Theban character.

Traditional Corner: The traditional corner is used to replace our Theban characters with your own if you don't want to use the ones presented in this workbook. Use this space to substitute with your own traditional characters and then use the rest of the workbook to help you learn to write the entire alphabet.

Traditional Corner

Theban Trace ™: The row of boxes below will contain the Theban letter. Use your pen or pencil and trace each one to get the feel of how the character is written. Use the 'How to write the character' as your reference.

***Theban Search*:** These are practice areas to help learn the letters you have just worked on. These Theban word search puzzles will really help your retention in learning these characters.

Character Retention

Flashcards are downloadable from our website to help with your studying of the Theban alphabet. Pick out the characters you have learned, and before you go to bed, go through them over and over again to help with the memorization process. When you have a little free time and you are away from this workbook, write out the characters you just learned, try forming some words, and sentences. Doing this daily will also help you remember the characters. As you go through this workbook, you will also notice that some of the roman characters are changed to reflect the Theban characters you have learned. When you have finished this workbook you should be able to read page 105 and the back cover of this book.

NOTE: The secret to learning the THEBAN - you must practice it daily until you can get a real good grasp of it.

SAMPLES
At the end of this workbook you will be given several samples from our book "**Theban Puzzle Workbook – Volume 1**", a continuation of learning Theban from this workbook. Once you have mastered the alphabet in this workbook, don't stop there, keep going!! You are opening a new door for yourself into the mystic world of THEBAN and we don't want you to lose it, but retain it.

BOOKS
You will have the chance to test your THEBAN skills in additional Theban Today workbooks, which are based on the characters used in this workbook, to help you retain what you've just learned. We just can't leave you hanging after completing this book. Visit **www.ThebanToday.com** for more information.

Website and Social Media

Please visit our website for additional information on Theban. There you will find more practice tools to help you continue learning this magickal alphabet. You can also join us on **Twitter**® at **www.Twitter.com/ThebanToday** and receive updates.

Bonus Theban Flash Cards

Once you complete the workbook and you want to continue to retain what you've learned, we found it helpful to use flash cards. If you would like a template to print out on your own computer, decode the message below to get your free flashcards.

Message in Theban For You

ᛁᛘᚻᚢᛘᚢᛇᛂᚲᛁᛇᛁᛁᚢᛘᚻᛒ ᚢᛘᛘ ᛂᛁᛊᚢᚻᚢ ᛂᚢᚲ ᛂᚢᛂᚲ ᚢᚻᛘ ᛘᚢᚢᛘᚢᚻᚢ ᛂᚢᚢᛒ
ᛂᚢᛒᛒᚢᚢᛘᚲ

ᛘᚢᚻᚢ ᛂᛘᚢ ᚢᚢᚲᚢ ᚢᚢᛒᛂᚢᛘᚢᛘ ᛂᚢᚢᛂᚢᚻ, ᛂᛘᚢ ᛘᚢᚻ ᚢᛘᚢᚢᛂᚢ ᛂᛘᚢᛘ ᚢᛘᛘᚲ
ᛘᚢᚢ ᛒᚢᚢᛘᛘᚢᛒ ᚢᚻᛘ ᛂᛘᚢᛘ ᛒᚢᚢᛇᛇᛒ ᚢᛘ ᛂᚢᚲ ᚢᛒᛒᚢᚢᛘᚢᛇ ᚢᚻᛘ ᛂᚢᚢᚢᛘᚲᚢᛇ
ᛒᛘᚢᚢᛒᛘ

ᛘᛂᚢᚢᛒᚢ ᚢᚢᛒᚢᛘ ᛘᛘᛘ ᚢᛂᚢᛒᛒᚢᛂᚢ ᚢᛒ ᚢᚢᚢᚢᛘᚲᛂᚢᚢᚢᚢᚻᛂᛘᛘᚢᛘᛒᚲᛘᛘᛒ ᚢᛘᛘ
ᛂᛘᚢᚢ ᚢᚻᛘᚢᛘᚢᛘᚢᛇᚢᛘᚻ ᛘᚻ ᚢᛘᚢ ᛂᚢ ᚢᚻᚢᛘᚻᚢᚢ ᛂᛘᚢᛘ ᛒᚲᚢᚢᛇᛇ ᚢᚻ
ᛘᚢᚢᛘᚢᚻᚢ ᚢᚻᛘ ᚢᛘᚢᚲᚢᚻᚢ ᛂᚢᚢᛒ ᛂᚢᚢᛂᚢᚻ ᛒᛘᚢᚢᛒᛘ   ᛂᚢ ᛘᛘᚢᚢᚻᚲᛘᛘᚢᛘ

ᛂᛘᛘᚢ ᛂᚢᚢᚢᚢᚻ ᚢᚲᚢᛒᚢ ᛘᚢᚢᛘᛒ, ᛘᛘᚢᚻ ᛂᛘᛘᚢ ᚢᚢᚢ ᚢᛘᛘᚢᛒᛂᚢᛘ ᚢᚻᛘ ᚢᚢ
ᛂᚢ ᚢᚢᚢᛒᚲᚢᚢᛘᛘᛘᛒ.ᛂᚢᚢᚢᚢᚻᛒᛘᛘᛘᚢᛒ.ᚢᛘᛘ   ᛂᚢᚲ ᚢᛒᚢᛘᛘᚲᚢᚢ ᚢᛒ:
ᛂᚢᚢᚢᚢᚻᛒᛘᛘᚢᛒ ᚢᚻᛘ ᛂᚢᚲ ᚢᚻᛒᛒᚢᛘᛘᛘ ᚢᛒ: ᚻᚢᛘᛂᚢᛒᛂᛘᛘ

How to Write the Character

ว   ภ   ฦ

Theban-Trace

Traditional Corner

Given Letter

ฦ ฦ ฦ ฦ ฦ ฦ ฦ ฦ

PRACTICE

A   A   A   A   A   A   A   A   A   A

A   A   A   A   A   A   A   A   A   A

A   A   A   A   A   A   A   A   A   A

A A A A A A A A A A

A A A A A A A A A A

A A A A A A A A A A

A A A A A A A A A A

A A A A A A A A A A

A A A A A A A A A A

How to Writꑘ thꑘ Chꑘrꑘctꑘr

Thꑘ bꑘ n – Trꑘ c ꑘ

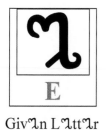

E

Givꑘn Lꑘttꑘr

Traditional Corner

PRꑘCTICꑘ

E   E   E   E   E   E   E   E   E   E

E   E   E   E   E   E   E   E   E   E

E   E   E   E   E   E   E   E   E   E

E	A	E	A	A	E	E	A	E	A

A	E	A	E	E	A	E	A	E	E

A	A	E	A	E	E	A	E	A	A

E	E	A	A	E	A	E	E	A	E

E	A	E	A	A	E	A	E	E	A

E	A	A	A	E	E	A	E	A	E

How to WrꞀtꞈ thꞈ ChꞀrꞀctꞈr

ThꞀ bꞀn – TrꞀ c ꞈ

U
I

GꞀvꞈn LꞀttꞈr

PRꞀCTꞀCꞈ

I   I   I   I   I   I   I   I   I

I   I   I   I   I   I   I   I   I

I   I   I   I   I   I   I   I   I

I   I   I   I   I   I   I   I   I   I

I   I   I   I   I   I   I   I   I   I

I   I   I   I   I   I   I   I   I   I

I   I   I   I   I   I   I   I   I   I

I   I   I   I   I   I   I   I   I   I

I   I   I   I   I   I   I   I   I   I

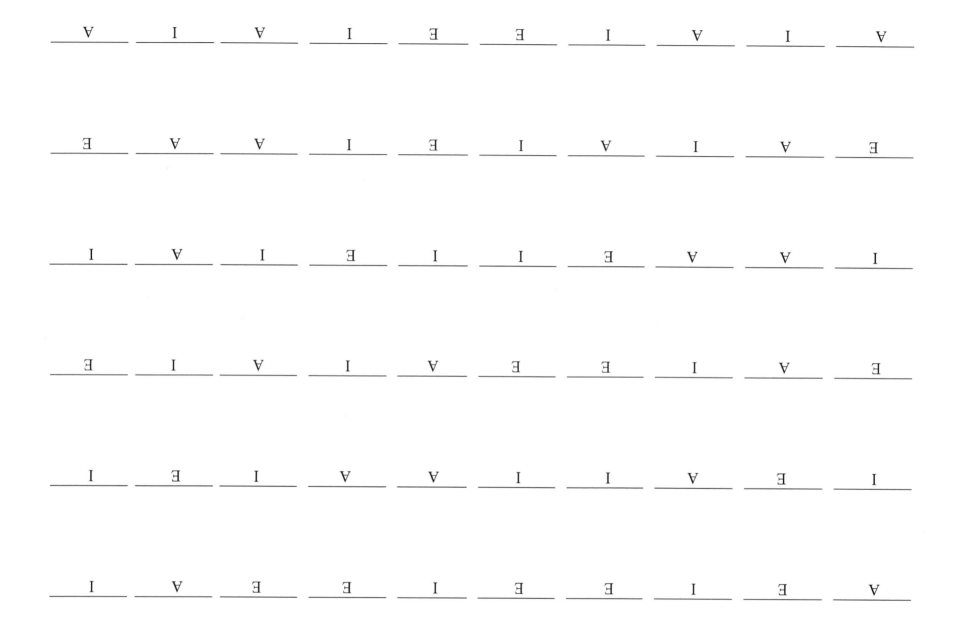

Hℳw tℒ WrƱtℒ thℒ Chℐrℳctℒr

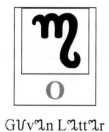

GƱvℒn Lℐttℒr

Thℒ bℐn – Trℐcℒ

PRℐCTƱCℒ

O   O   O   O   O   O   O   O   O   O

O   O   O   O   O   O   O   O   O   O

O   O   O   O   O   O   O   O   O   O

Traditional Corner

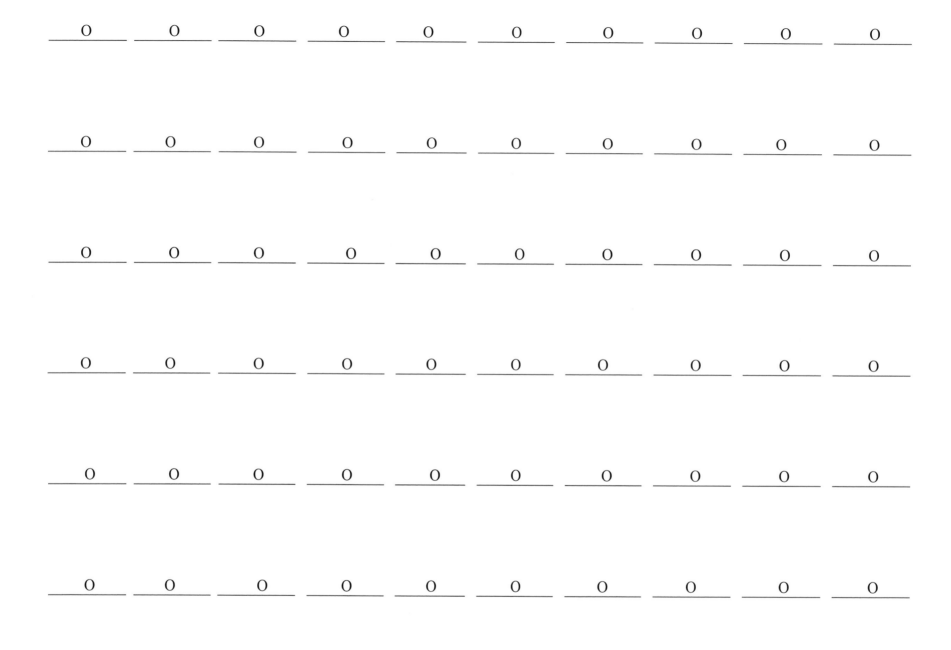

A	I	E	O	I	A	A	I	O	E
E	O	O	E	I	A	O	A	O	E
O	I	E	O	A	I	E	O	I	A
I	O	E	O	A	I	O	I	A	E
A	E	I	O	O	I	E	A	O	I
E	A	I	O	I	A	O	E	O	I

H℧w tɁ WrႱtɁ thɁ ChႱrɁctɁr

GႱvɁn LɁttɁr

U

Traditional Corner

ThɁ bႱn – TrɁ c Ɂ

PRႱCTႱCɁ

U	U	U	U	U	U	U	U	U	U
U	U	U	U	U	U	U	U	U	U
U	U	U	U	U	U	U	U	U	U

U	U	U	U	U	U	U	U	U	U
U	U	U	U	U	U	U	U	U	U
U	U	U	U	U	U	U	U	U	U
U	U	U	U	U	U	U	U	U	U
U	U	U	U	U	U	U	U	U	U
U	U	U	U	U	U	U	U	U	U

I	E	U	A	U	O	A	I	U	E
A	U	E	U	I	U	O	U	O	E
E	U	I	A	O	U	A	I	E	U
I	U	O	U	A	E	I	U	E	U
O	U	E	E	O	U	A	O	U	I
A	U	O	E	U	I	A	I	U	O

Hꙗw tꙗ WrꙊtꙗ thꙗ Chꙗrꙗctꙗr

B

GꙊvꙗn Lꙗttꙗr

Thꙗꙙ n – Trꙗ c ꙗ

PRꙗCTꙊCꙗ

B	B	B	B	B	B	B	B	B
B	B	B	B	B	B	B	B	B
B	B	B	B	B	B	B	B	B

Traditional Corner

B   B   B   B   B   B   B   B   B   B

B   B   B   B   B   B   B   B   B   B

B   B   B   B   B   B   B   B   B   B

B   B   B   B   B   B   B   B   B   B

B   B   B   B   B   B   B   B   B   B

B   B   B   B   B   B   B   B   B   B

A	E	I	U	B	O	E	B	A	I

B	A	U	B	I	E	U	O	A	B

E	O	B	A	I	O	E	B	A	I

I	A	B	I	U	A	O	A	B	E

O	U	B	A	E	A	I	O	U	A

B	I	E	U	A	B	O	U	A	I

Ꟁ Ɣ _C_ D ꟾ F G H Ʊ J K L M N ꟽ P Q R S T Ỿ V W X Y Z .

Thꟾꟾꟾ n - Trꟾꟾꟾ

PRꟾꟽTʊꟽꟾ

Gʊvꟾn Lꟾttꟾr

C

Traditional Corner

C   C   C   C   C   C   C   C   C   C

C   C   C   C   C   C   C   C   C   C

C   C   C   C   C   C   C   C   C   C

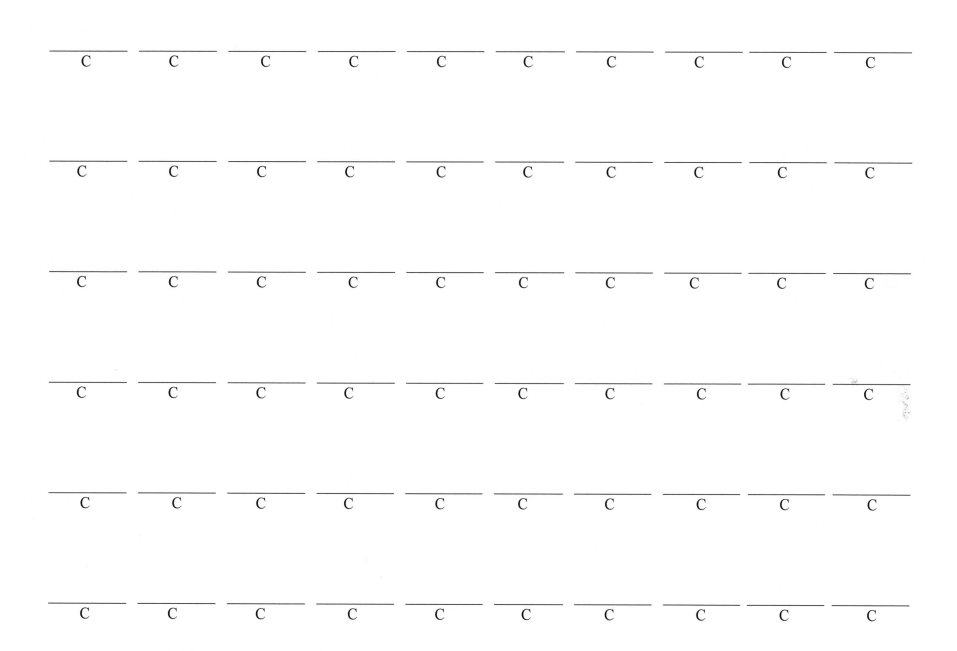

A	E	I	U	C	O	E	B	A	I
C	A	U	B	I	E	U	O	A	C
E	O	B	A	I	O	E	C	A	I
I	A	C	I	U	A	O	A	C	E
C	U	B	A	E	A	I	O	U	A
B	I	E	U	A	C	O	U	A	I

Hᛖwtᛖ Wrᚢtᛖ thᛖ ᛚhᛁrᛁᛚtᛖr

Thᚨᛖᛁ n - Trᛁᛖᛚ

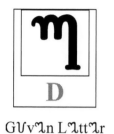

D

Gᚢvᛁn Lᛁttᛖr

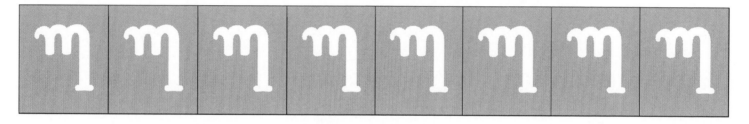

Traditional Corner

PRᛁᛚTᚢᛚᛁ

| D | D | D | D | D | D | D | D | D | D |

| D | D | D | D | D | D | D | D | D | D |

| D | D | D | D | D | D | D | D | D | D |

D   D   D   D   D   D   D   D   D   D

D   D   D   D   D   D   D   D   D   D

D   D   D   D   D   D   D   D   D   D

D   D   D   D   D   D   D   D   D   D

D   D   D   D   D   D   D   D   D   D

D   D   D   D   D   D   D   D   D   D

A   E   D   U   C   O   E   B   A   I

C   A   U   B   I   E   U   O   D   C

E   O   B   D   D   O   E   C   A   I

I   A   D   I   U   D   O   A   C   E

C   D   B   A   E   A   I   O   U   A

B   I   E   U   A   C   O   U   A   D

Hꑰw tꑰ Wrꎙtꑰ thꑰ ꎙhꑰrꑰꎙtꑰr

Thꑰꑭꑴ n - Trꑭꑰꑴ

PRꑭꎙTUꎙꑴ

Traditional Corner

F   F   F   F   F   F   F   F   F   F

F   F   F   F   F   F   F   F   F   F

F   F   F   F   F   F   F   F   F   F

F   F   F   F   F   F   F   F   F   F

F   F   F   F   F   F   F   F   F   F

F   F   F   F   F   F   F   F   F   F

F   F   F   F   F   F   F   F   F   F

F   F   F   F   F   F   F   F   F   F

F   F   F   F   F   F   F   F   F   F

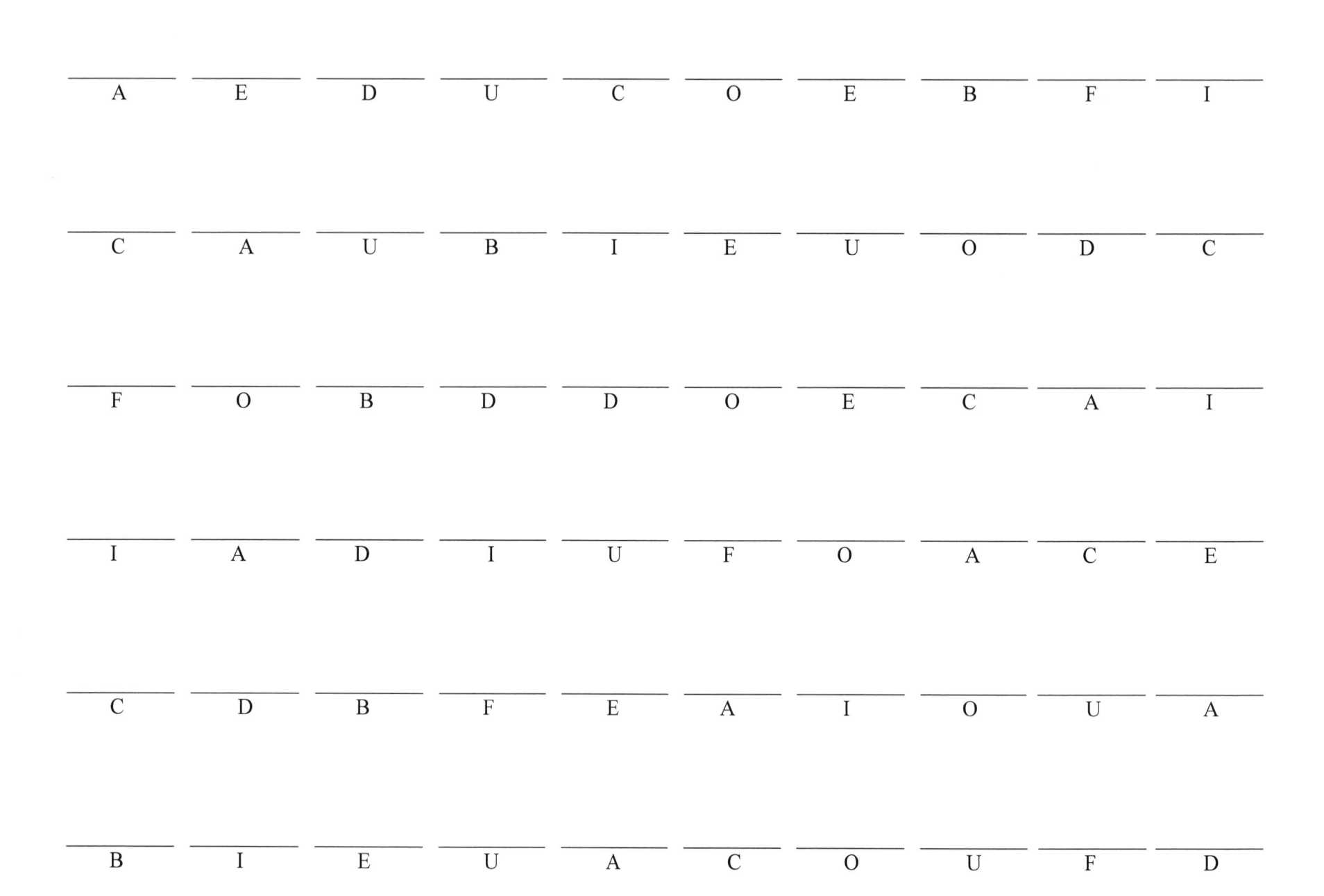

A	E	D	U	C	O	E	B	F	I
C	A	U	B	I	E	U	O	D	C
F	O	B	D	D	O	E	C	A	I
I	A	D	I	U	F	O	A	C	E
C	D	B	F	E	A	I	O	U	A
B	I	E	U	A	C	O	U	F	D

THEBAN SEARCH 1

BEAD   **BOO**   **COD**   **DAD**   **DEAD**

DECAF   **DEFACED**   **FACE**   **FADE**   **FEE**

ꙗꙙꙗꙙꙙ**_GH_**ꙂꙨ**J K L M N**ꙙ**P Q R S T**ꙗ**V W X Y Z .**

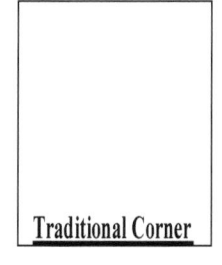
Traditional Corner

ꙂꙨvꙙn Lꙙttꙙr
G

Thꙙ4ꙗ n - Trꙗꙗꙙ

PRꙗꙗTꙨꙗꙙ

G	G	G	G	G	G	G	G	G	G
G	G	G	G	G	G	G	G	G	G
G	G	G	G	G	G	G	G	G	G

G   G   G   G   G   G   G   G   G   G

G   G   G   G   G   G   G   G   G   G

G   G   G   G   G   G   G   G   G   G

G   G   G   G   G   G   G   G   G   G

G   G   G   G   G   G   G   G   G   G

G   G   G   G   G   G   G   G   G   G

I	A	G	I	U	F	O	A	C	E

C	D	B	F	E	G	I	O	G	A

G	I	E	U	A	G	O	U	F	D

A	E	D	U	C	O	E	B	F	I

C	A	U	B	I	E	G	O	D	C

F	G	B	D	D	O	E	C	A	G

THEBAN SEARCH 2

ADDED   **BAD**   **BAGGED**   **BEEF**   **BUGGED**

DUBBED   **DUDE**   **FEED**   **FIG**   **GOOD**

ᚦᚥw tᚾ Wrᚢtᚱ tᚦᚱ ᚾᚦᚱᚾᚥtᚱr

Tᚦᚱᚴᚦ n - Trᚾᚦᚾ

PRᚾᚥTᚢᚥᚱ

'ᚢᚢvᚱn Lᚱttᚱr

H

Traditional Corner

H   H   H   H   H   H   H   H   H   H

H   H   H   H   H   H   H   H   H   H

H   H   H   H   H   H   H   H   H   H

H   H   H   H   H   H   H   H   H   H

H   H   H   H   H   H   H   H   H   H

H   H   H   H   H   H   H   H   H   H

H   H   H   H   H   H   H   H   H   H

H   H   H   H   H   H   H   H   H   H

H   H   H   H   H   H   H   H   H   H

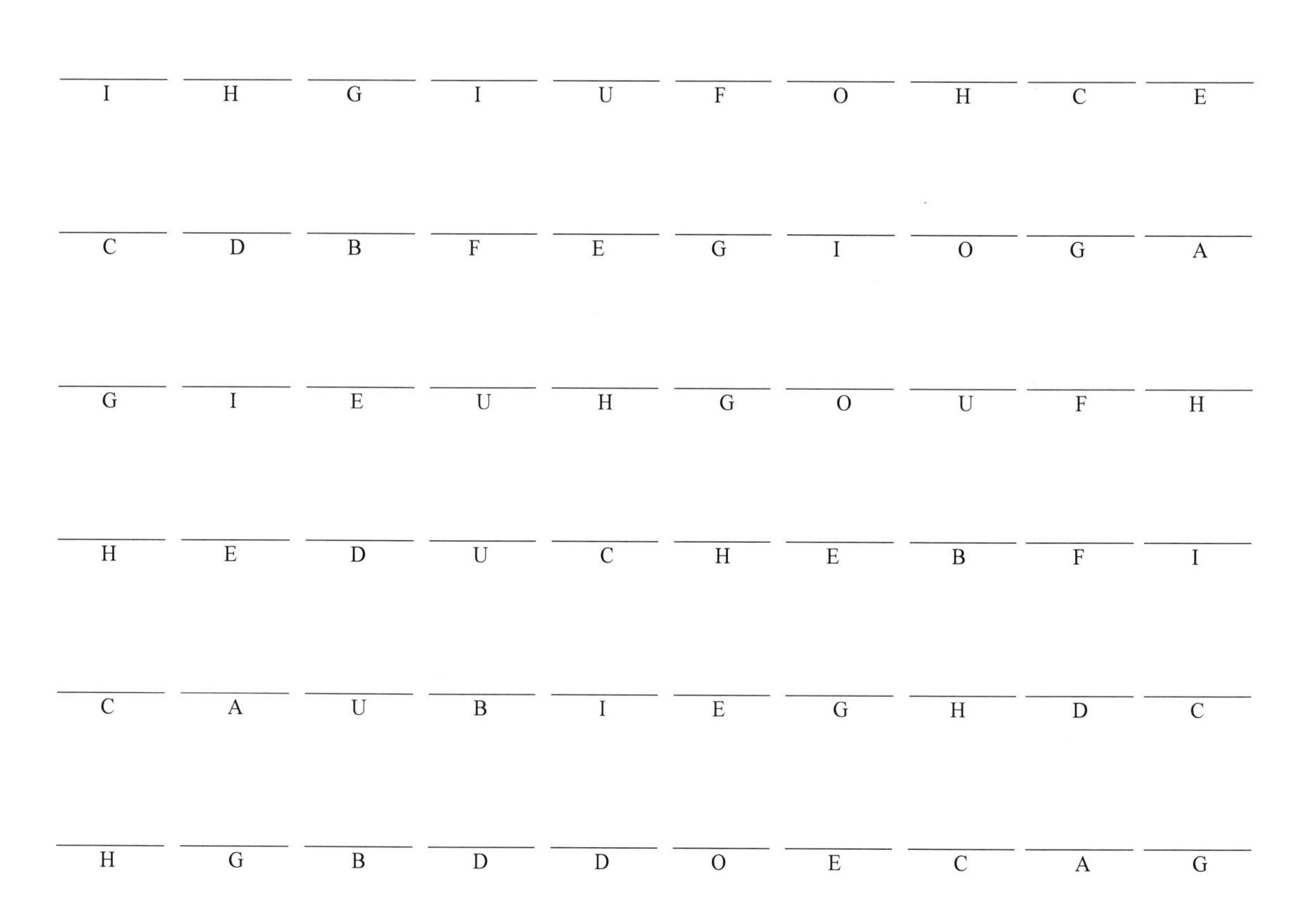

I   H   G   I   U   F   O   H   C   E

C   D   B   F   E   G   I   O   G   A

G   I   E   U   H   G   O   U   F   H

H   E   D   U   C   H   E   B   F   I

C   A   U   B   I   E   G   H   D   C

H   G   B   D   D   O   E   C   A   G

THEBAN SEARCH 3

ℳ ᵯ ᵴ ᵯ ᵯ ᵯ ᵯ ᵯ ℗ ᵯ
ᵮ ᵯ ᵯ ᵯ ᵱ ᵯ ᵯ ᵯ ᵯ ᵯ
ᵯ ᵯ ᵯ ᵮ ᵱ ᵱ ᵱ ᵯ ᵱ ᵮ
ᵯ ᵱ ᵱ ᵱ ᵯ ᵱ ᵯ ᵯ ᵶ ᵱ
ᵯ ᵱ ᵮ ℗ ᵯ ᵯ ᵯ ᵯ ᵮ ᵮ
ᵮ ᵮ ᵯ ᵮ ᵱ ᵮ ᵯ ᵯ ᵴ ᵯ
ᵯ ᵴ ᵯ ᵯ ᵱ ᵯ ᵮ ᵯ ᵱ ᵴ
ᵯ ᵯ ᵯ ᵯ ᵯ ᵶ ᵹ ᵯ ᵯ ℨ
ᵯ ᵹ ᵶ ᵯ ᵯ ᵹ ᵯ ᵹ ᵮ ᵱ
ᵮ ᵯ ᵱ ᵱ ᵱ ᵱ ᵮ ᵱ ᵯ ℗

BADGE	BOGIE	BOOGIE	COUGH	DODGE	DOGGED
DOUGH	FUDGE	GOOD	HIGH	HOG	HUGGED

ꟼꟺw tꟼ WrUtꟼ tꟼꟼ ꟼꟼrꟼꟺtꟼr

J

UUvꟼn Lꟼttꟼr

Tꟼꟼꟼꟼ n - Trꟼꟼꟼ

PRꟼꟺTUꟺꟼ

J J J J J J J J J J

J J J J J J J J J J

J J J J J J J J J J

| J | J | J | J | J | J | J | J | J | J |

| J | J | J | J | J | J | J | J | J | J |

| J | J | J | J | J | J | J | J | J | J |

| J | J | J | J | J | J | J | J | J | J |

| J | J | J | J | J | J | J | J | J | J |

| J | J | J | J | J | J | J | J | J | J |

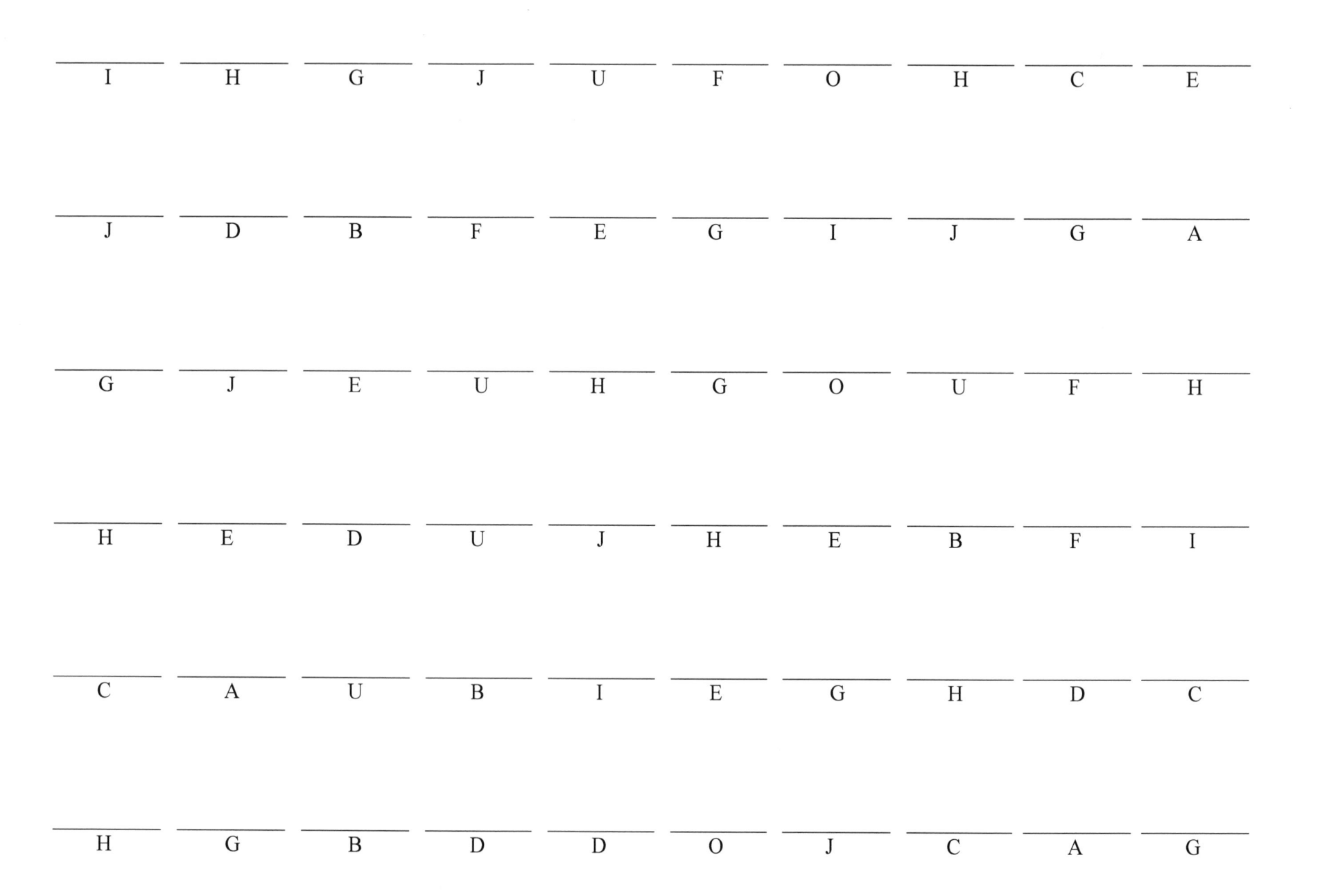

I	H	G	J	U	F	O	H	C	E
J	D	B	F	E	G	I	J	G	A
G	J	E	U	H	G	O	U	F	H
H	E	D	U	J	H	E	B	F	I
C	A	U	B	I	E	G	H	D	C
H	G	B	D	D	O	J	C	A	G

THEBAN SEARCH 4

AGED   **DEAF**   **DOUG**   **FIJI**   **JABBED**

JACOB   **JADED**   **JEFF**   **JOG**   **JUDGE**

ᚸᚸw tᚸ Wrᚸtᚸ tᚸᚸ ᚸᚸᚸrᚸᚸtᚸr

K

ᚸᚸvᚸn Lᚸttᚸr

Tᚸᚸᚸᚸ n - Trᚸᚸᚸ

Traditional Corner

PRᚸᚸTᚸᚸᚸ

| K | K | K | K | K | K | K | K | K | K |

| K | K | K | K | K | K | K | K | K | K |

| K | K | K | K | K | K | K | K | K | K |

___ K ___ K ___ K ___ K ___ K ___ K ___ K ___ K ___ K ___ K

___ K ___ K ___ K ___ K ___ K ___ K ___ K ___ K ___ K ___ K

___ K ___ K ___ K ___ K ___ K ___ K ___ K ___ K ___ K ___ K

___ K ___ K ___ K ___ K ___ K ___ K ___ K ___ K ___ K ___ K

___ K ___ K ___ K ___ K ___ K ___ K ___ K ___ K ___ K ___ K

___ K ___ K ___ K ___ K ___ K ___ K ___ K ___ K ___ K ___ K

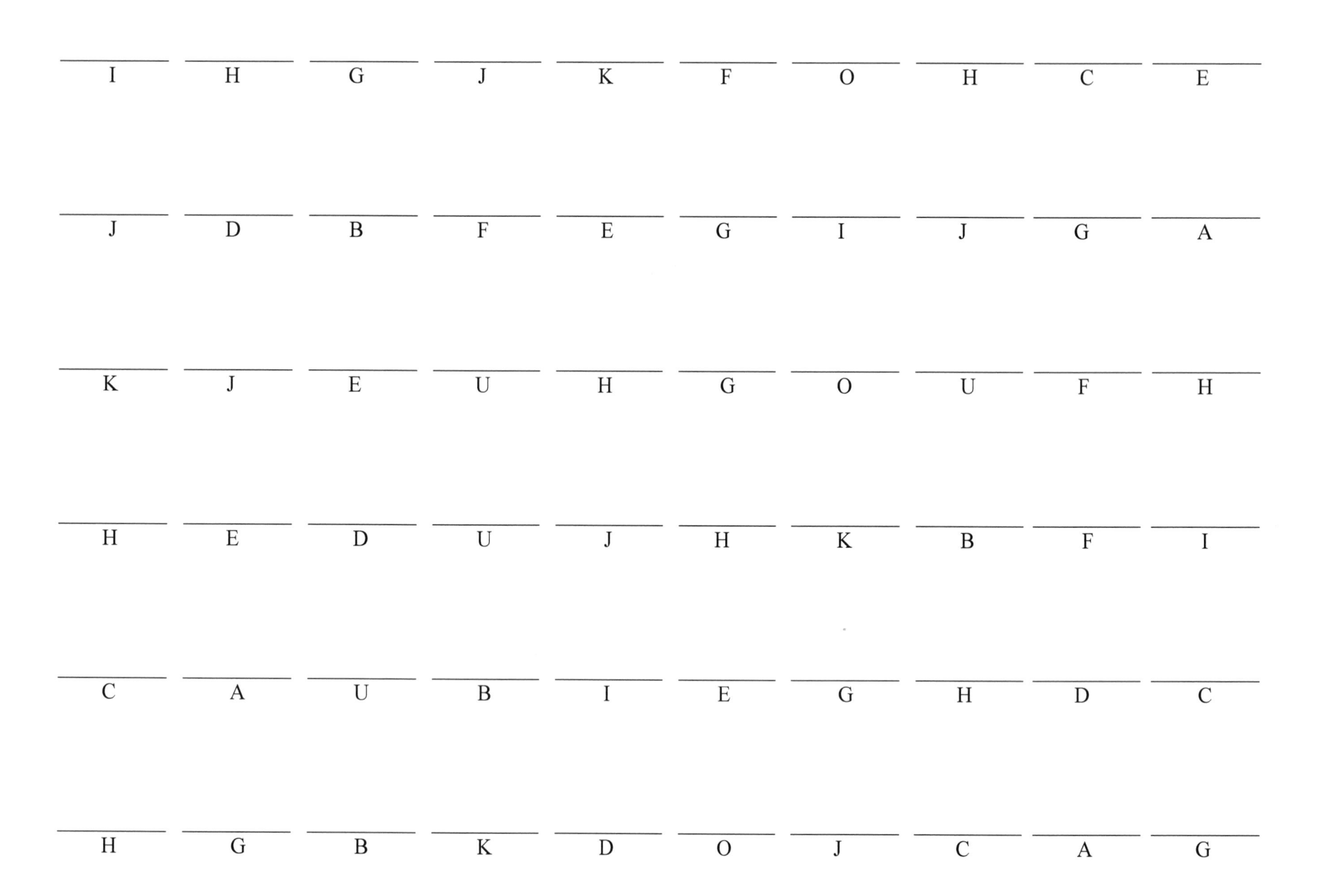

I   H   G   J   K   F   O   H   C   E

J   D   B   F   E   G   I   J   G   A

K   J   E   U   H   G   O   U   F   H

H   E   D   U   J   H   K   B   F   I

C   A   U   B   I   E   G   H   D   C

H   G   B   K   D   O   J   C   A   G

THEBAN SEARCH 5

BAKE   BED   CAGE   CAKE   COKE   DECK

DOCK   DUKE   FAKE   JACK   JOKE   KID

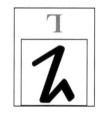

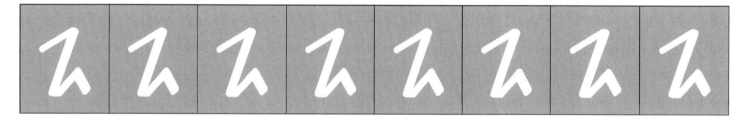

ZYXWV∨UTSRQPⁿNMLⱡⱡⱡⱡⱡⱡⱡⱡⱡⱡⱡ

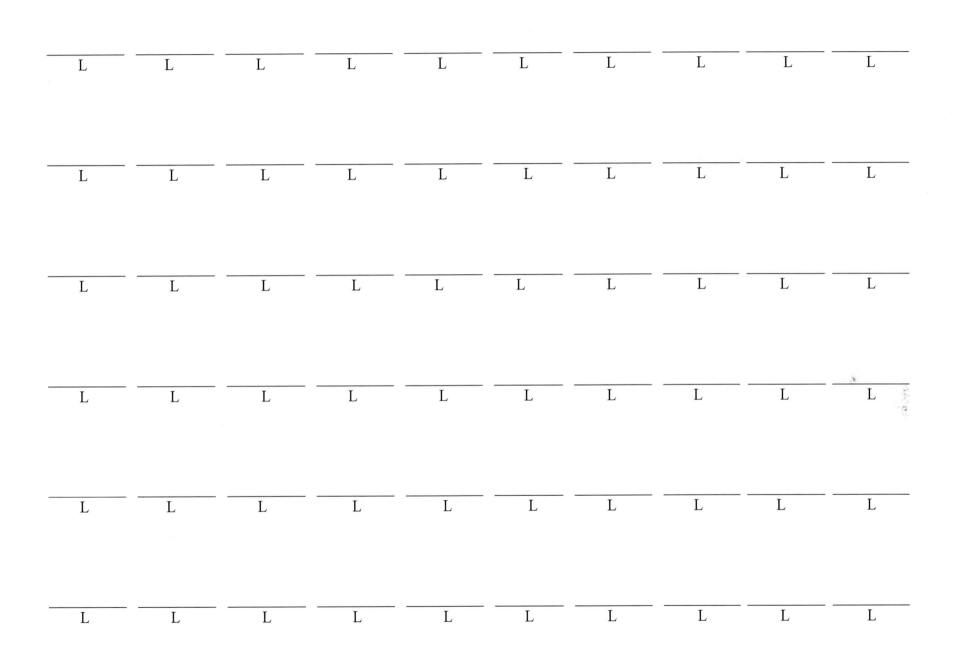

H	E	D	U	L	H	K	B	F	I
C	A	U	B	I	E	G	H	D	L
H	G	B	K	L	O	J	C	A	G
I	H	G	J	K	F	O	H	C	E
J	D	B	F	E	G	I	L	G	A
K	J	E	U	H	G	O	U	F	H
L	A	B	I	E	D	L	K	J	H

THEBAN SEARCH 6

DOGFOOD **DOLL** **GOOFBALL** **HAIL** **HOLD**
LAUGH **LOAD** **LOCK** **LOOK** **LOUD**

ᚦᚦw tᚦ Wrᚢtᚦ tᚦᚦ ᚦᚦᚦrᚦᚦtᚦr

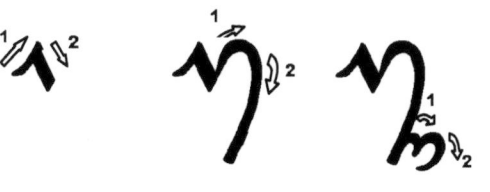

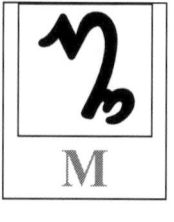

M

ᚢᚢvᚦn ᚦᚦttᚦr

Tᚦᚦᚦᚦ n - Trᚦᚦᚦ

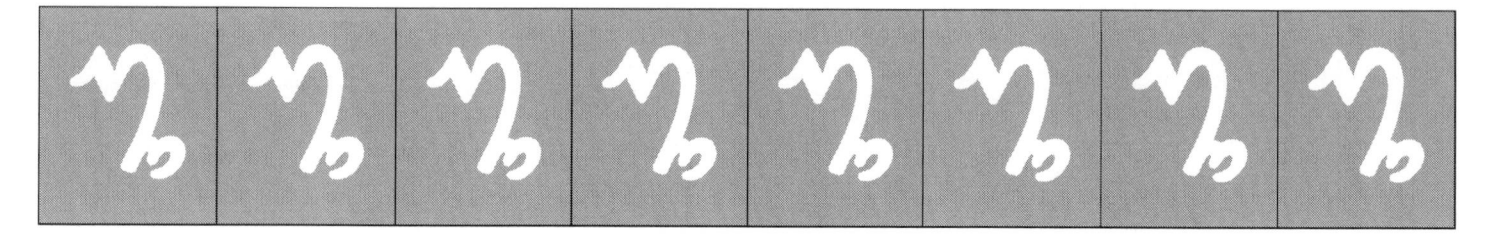

PRᚦᚦTᚢᚦᚦ

M	M	M	M	M	M	M	M	M
M	M	M	M	M	M	M	M	M
M	M	M	M	M	M	M	M	M

M	M	M	M	M	M	M	M	M	M
M	M	M	M	M	M	M	M	M	M
M	M	M	M	M	M	M	M	M	M
M	M	M	M	M	M	M	M	M	M
M	M	M	M	M	M	M	M	M	M
M	M	M	M	M	M	M	M	M	M

H	M	D	U	L	H	K	B	F	I
C	A	U	B	I	E	G	M	M	L
H	M	B	K	L	M	J	C	M	G
M	H	M	J	K	F	O	H	C	E
M	D	B	F	M	G	I	L	M	A
K	J	E	U	H	G	O	U	F	H
L	A	B	I	E	D	L	K	M	U

THEBAN SEARCH 7

η ຂ Ч Ϥ ੧ ℔ ຖ U Z ੧
U Ϥ ຖ ຖ ℔℔ ℔ ℂ ຖ ੧ ຖ
Ϥ ੧ ੧ ຖ ຖ ੧ ℂ ੧ ੧ ຖ
ຖ U ຂ ຖ U ੧ ຂ Ϥ ੧ Ϥ
℔ ੧ Z U ຖ ੧ ຖ ੧ ຂ ຖ
U ຖ Ϥ ຖ Z ੧ ຖ ຖ U ℔
ຖ Ϥ ੧ Ϥ δ ℂ Γ Z ੧ U
℔℔ Z ℂ Z ੧ Ϥ ຖ ੧ ຖ ℔
℔℔ U ຂ ੧ Z U ຂ ຂ ℔℔ ຂ
Ϥ ຖ ຂ ੧ ℔ Ϥ ੧ ℔ ℔℔

BEEFCAKE   **CABBAGE**   **CHALK**   **DEBACLE**   **GOLD**
HOME   **MEAL**   **MILK**   **MODEL**   **MOLD**

ꝩꝩw tꝩ Wrꝯtꝩ tꝩꝩ ꝩꝩꝩrꝩꝩtꝩr

Tꝩꝩꝗꝩꝩ - Trꝩꝩꝩ

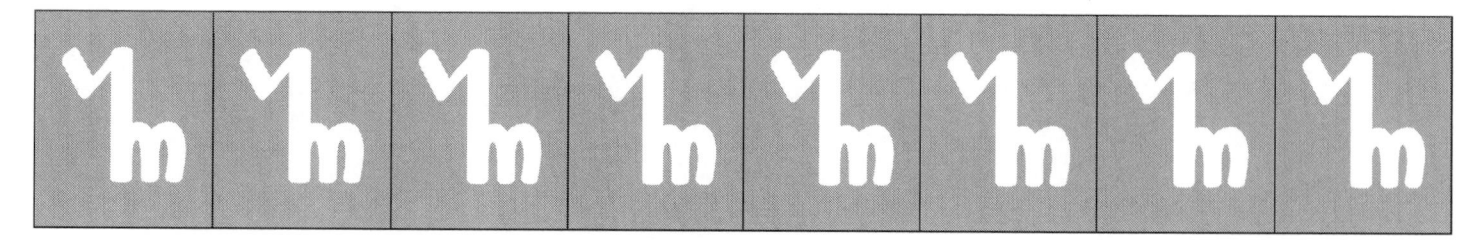

N

ꝩꝯꝯvꝩꝩ ꝩꝩttꝩr

PRꝩꝩTꝯꝩꝩ

N	N	N	N	N	N	N	N	N	N
N	N	N	N	N	N	N	N	N	N
N	N	N	N	N	N	N	N	N	N

N   N   N   N   N   N   N   N   N   N

N   N   N   N   N   N   N   N   N   N

N   N   N   N   N   N   N   N   N   N

N   N   N   N   N   N   N   N   N   N

N   N   N   N   N   N   N   N   N   N

N   N   N   N   N   N   N   N   N   N

__ H __ M __ D __ U __ L __ H __ K __ N __ F __ I

__ C __ A __ U __ B __ I __ E __ G __ M __ D __ L

__ N __ G __ B __ K __ L __ M __ J __ C __ M __ G

__ I __ H __ G __ J __ K __ N __ O __ H __ C __ E

__ M __ D __ B __ F __ M __ G __ I __ L __ M __ A

__ K __ J __ E __ U __ H __ G __ O __ U __ F __ N

__ L __ A __ B __ I __ N __ D __ L __ K __ O __ U

THEBAN SEARCH 8

BIKING   **CHAIN**   **DIAMOND**   **FLAG**   **HAMMOCK**

LANDING   **MOON**   **NICKEL**   **NOODLE**   **NOON**

৵ৼw t৵ Wrৼtৼ t৵ৼ ৵৵ৼrৼৼtৼr

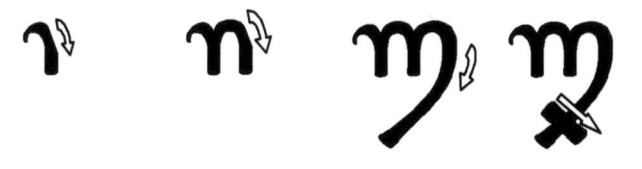

Tৼৼৼৼ - Trৼৼৼ

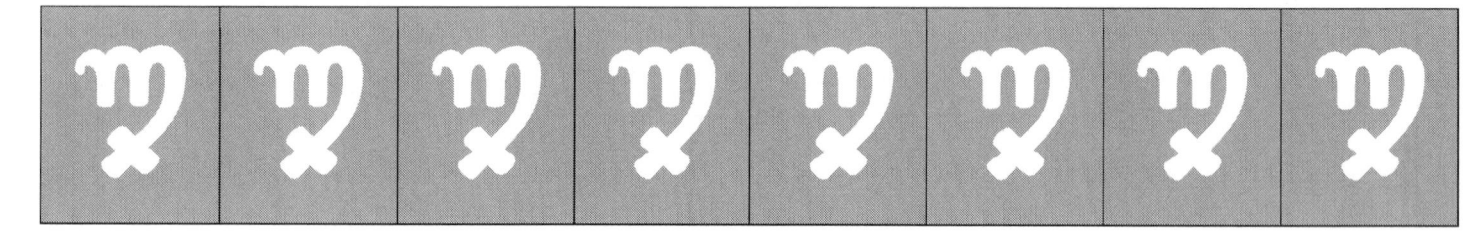

ৼRৼৼTৼৼৼ

P	P	P	P	P	P	P	P	P
P	P	P	P	P	P	P	P	P
P	P	P	P	P	P	P	P	P

Traditional Corner

P	P	P	P	P	P	P	P	P	P
P	P	P	P	P	P	P	P	P	P
P	P	P	P	P	P	P	P	P	P
P	P	P	P	P	P	P	P	P	P
P	P	P	P	P	P	P	P	P	P
P	P	P	P	P	P	P	P	P	P

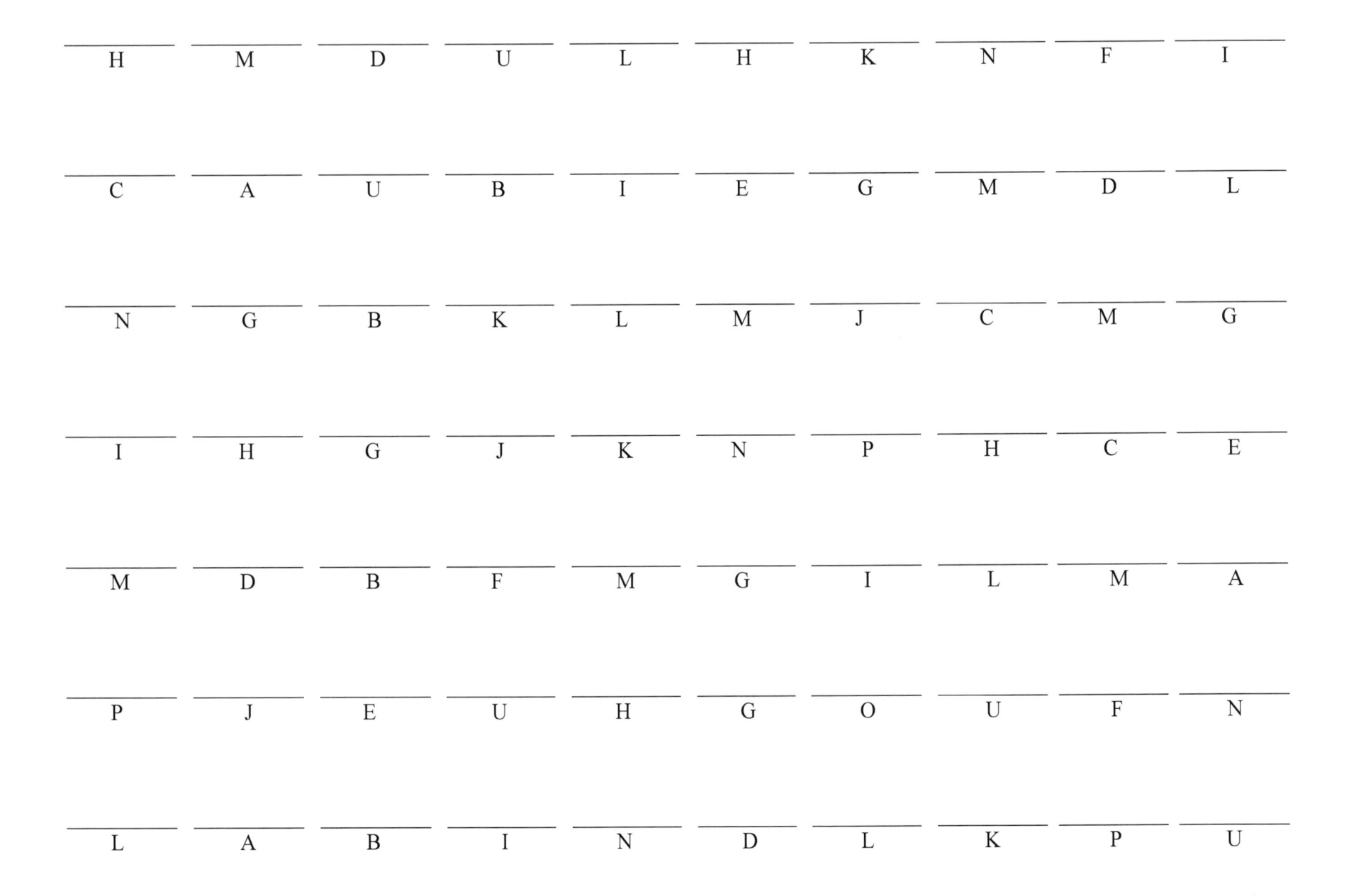

THEBAN SEARCH 9

CHICKEN   **DUMP**   **HAPPEN**   **JAPAN**   **JUMPING**

NAPKIN   **PINK**   **PLAN**   **PLUMP**   **POUND**

ꝣꝩw tꝩ Wrꝩtꝲ tꝩꝲ ꝩꝣꝩrꝩꝩtꝲr

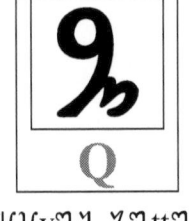

Q

ꝩꝩꝩvꝲꝥ ꝲꝲttꝲr

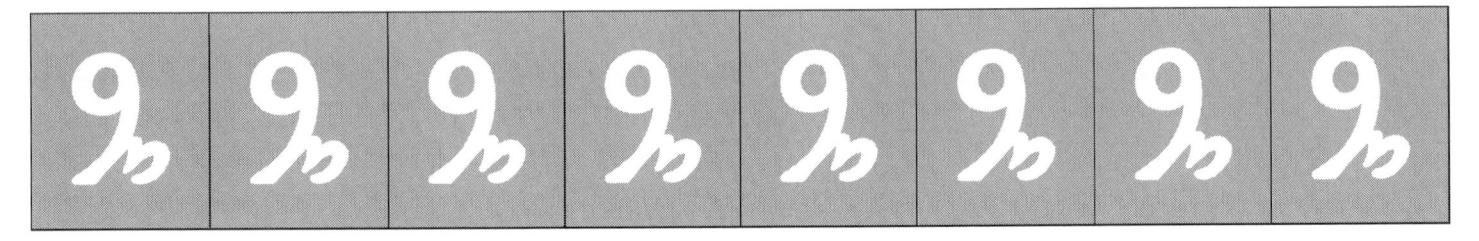

Tꝩꝲꝙꝩꝥ - Trꝩꝩꝲ

ꝥRꝩꝩTꝩꝩꝲ

Q	Q	Q	Q	Q	Q	Q	Q	Q	Q

Q	Q	Q	Q	Q	Q	Q	Q	Q	Q

Q	Q	Q	Q	Q	Q	Q	Q	Q	Q

Traditional Corner

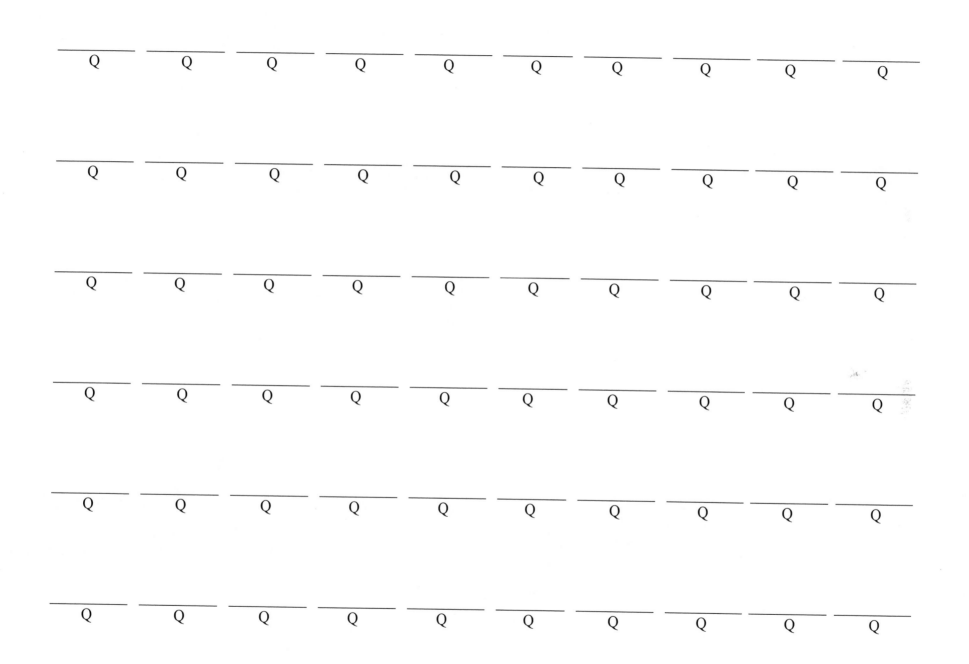

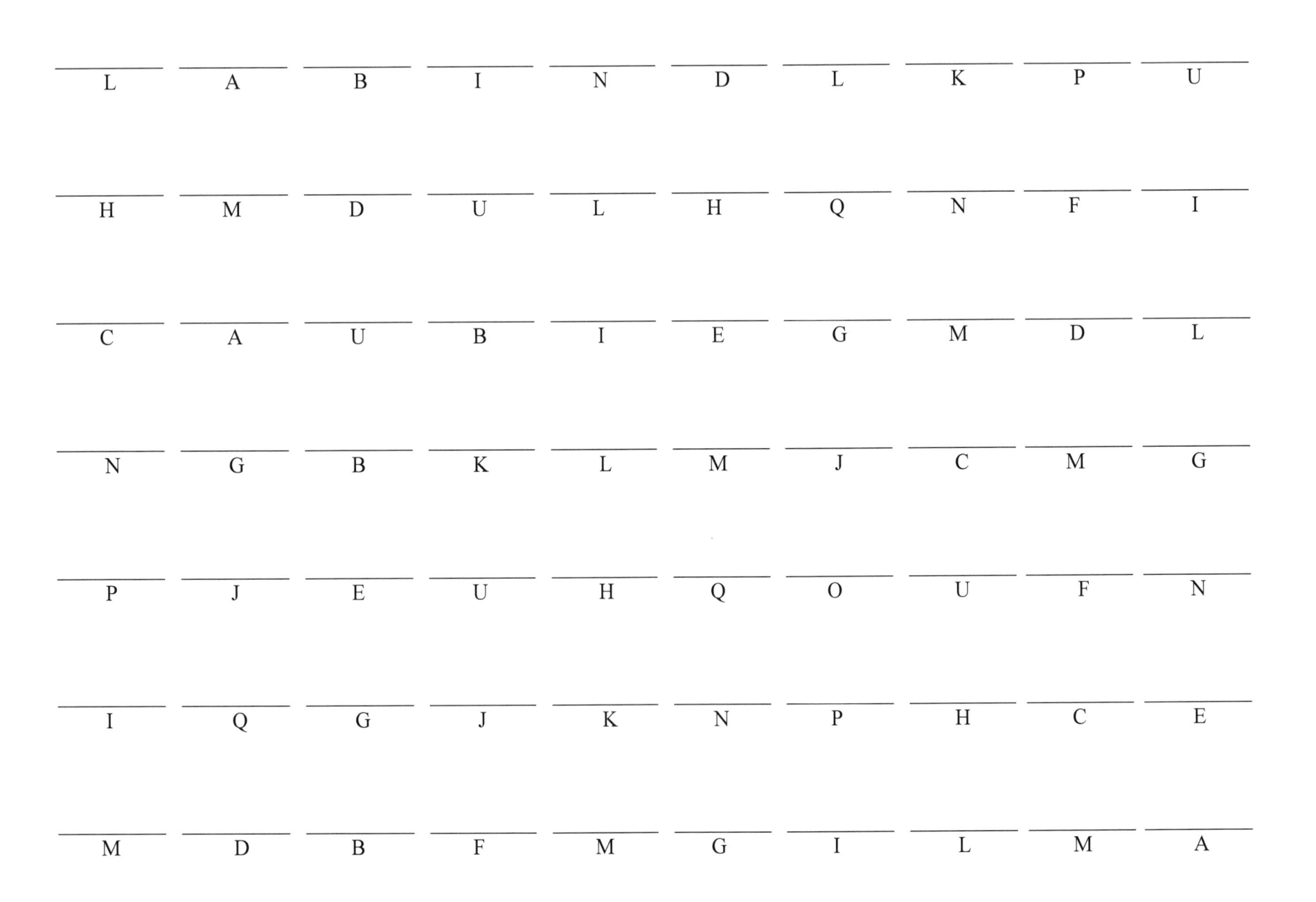

L	A	B	I	N	D	L	K	P	U
H	M	D	U	L	H	Q	N	F	I
C	A	U	B	I	E	G	M	D	L
N	G	B	K	L	M	J	C	M	G
P	J	E	U	H	Q	O	U	F	N
I	Q	G	J	K	N	P	H	C	E
M	D	B	F	M	G	I	L	M	A

THEBAN SEARCH 10

CINQUE   CLAQUE   CLIQUE   MANQUE   PLAQUE
QUACK   QUARK   QUEEN   QUICK   QUINCE

ꙩꙮw t ꟽ Wꟿꙋtꙉ tꙩꙉ ꙩꙗꙮꙗꟽtꙉꟽ

R

ꙓꙋꙋvꙉꙮ ꙉꙉttꙉꟽ

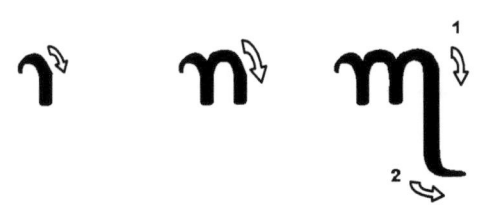

Tꙩꙉꙩꙮ - Tꟿꙉꙩꙉ

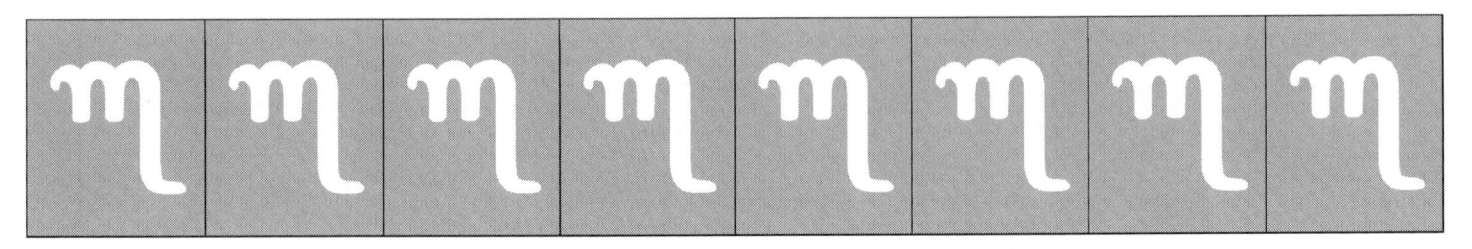

ꙮꟿꙉꙗꟿTꙋꙮꙉ

Traditional Corner

R	R	R	R	R	R	R	R	R	R

R	R	R	R	R	R	R	R	R	R

R	R	R	R	R	R	R	R	R	R

R _____ R _____ R _____ R _____ R _____ R _____ R _____ R _____ R _____ R _____

R _____ R _____ R _____ R _____ R _____ R _____ R _____ R _____ R _____ R _____

R _____ R _____ R _____ R _____ R _____ R _____ R _____ R _____ R _____ R _____

R _____ R _____ R _____ R _____ R _____ R _____ R _____ R _____ R _____ R _____

R _____ R _____ R _____ R _____ R _____ R _____ R _____ R _____ R _____ R _____

R _____ R _____ R _____ R _____ R _____ R _____ R _____ R _____ R _____ R _____

R   Q   G   J   K   N   P   H   C   E

P   J   E   U   H   Q   O   U   F   N

M   D   B   F   M   G   I   L   M   A

C   A   U   B   R   E   G   M   D   L

N   G   B   K   L   M   J   C   M   R

H   M   D   U   L   H   Q   N   F   I

R   A   B   I   N   D   L   K   P   U

THEBAN SEARCH 11

BEAR   **FARMLAND**   **FIGURE**   **FOUR**   **GEORGE**
PREQUEL   **RACE**   **RANGER**   **RAPID**   **ROBIN**

ᚽᛌw t ᛉ Wᛉᚢtᛉ tᚿᛉ ᛌᚿᚽᛉᚿᛌtᛉᛉ

Tᚿᛉᚽᛌᛄ - Tᛉᛌᚿᛉ

ᛉᛉᛌᛌTᛌᚢᛌᛉ

Traditional Corner

ᛌᛌᚡᛉᛆ ᛉᛉttᛉᛌ

S

S   S   S   S   S   S   S   S   S   S

S   S   S   S   S   S   S   S   S   S

S   S   S   S   S   S   S   S   S   S

S   S   S   S   S   S   S   S   S   S

S   S   S   S   S   S   S   S   S   S

S   S   S   S   S   S   S   S   S   S

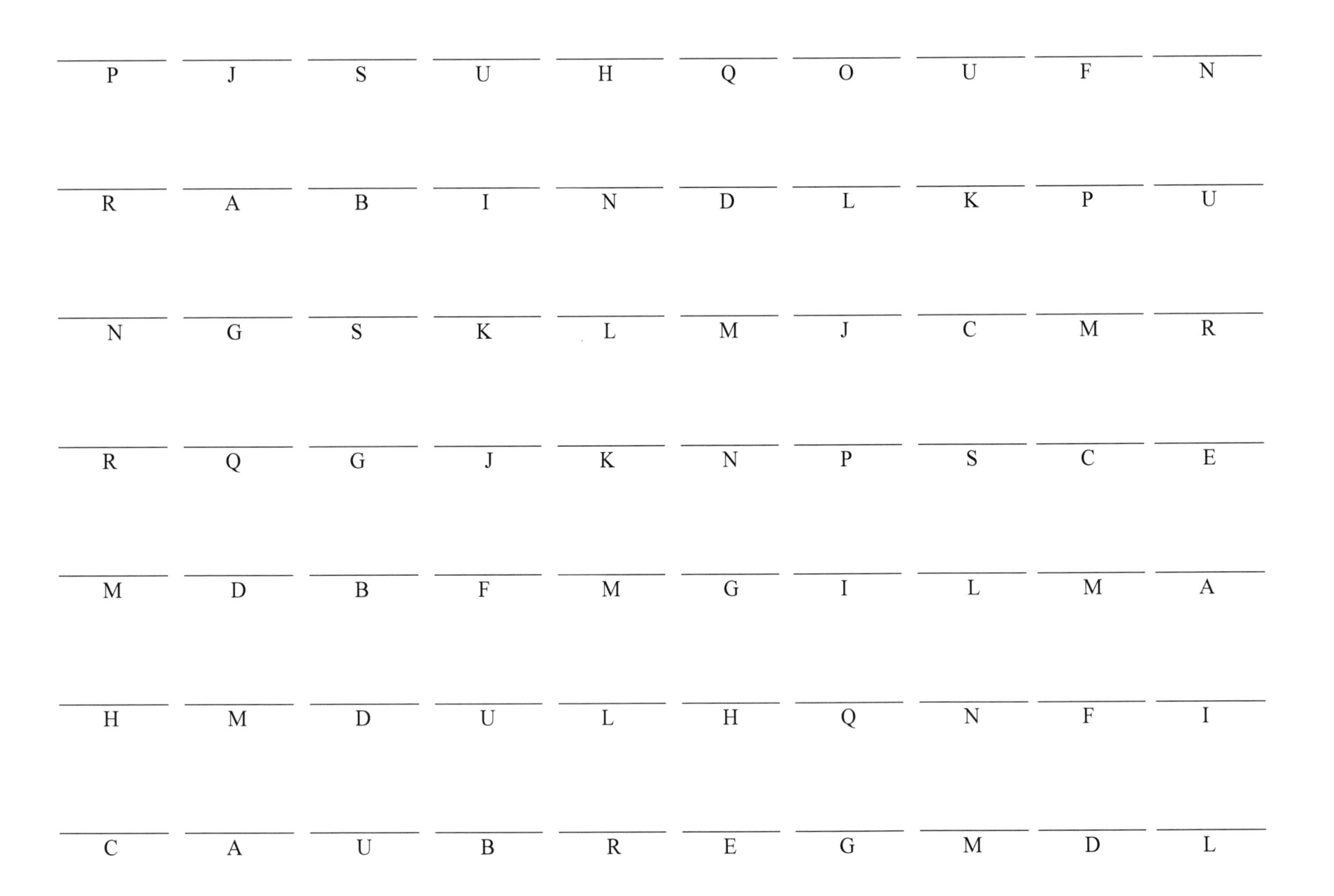

P   J   S   U   H   Q   O   U   F   N

R   A   B   I   N   D   L   K   P   U

N   G   S   K   L   M   J   C   M   R

R   Q   G   J   K   N   P   S   C   E

M   D   B   F   M   G   I   L   M   A

H   M   D   U   L   H   Q   N   F   I

C   A   U   B   R   E   G   M   D   L

THEBAN SEARCH 12

BUSINESS **CIRCUS** **CLASS** **MOONBEAMS** **SAMURAI**
SARDINES **SCALLOPS** **SEARCH** **SHOPPING** **SINGER**

ㄹㅁw ㄹㄹ W ㄹㅂㄹㄹ ㄹㄹㄹ ㄹㄹㄹㄹㄹㄹㄹ

Traditional Corner

ㄴㄴㄴㄹㄹ ㄹㄹㄹㄹㄹ

ㄹㄹㄹㄹㄹㄹ - ㄹㄹㄹㄹ

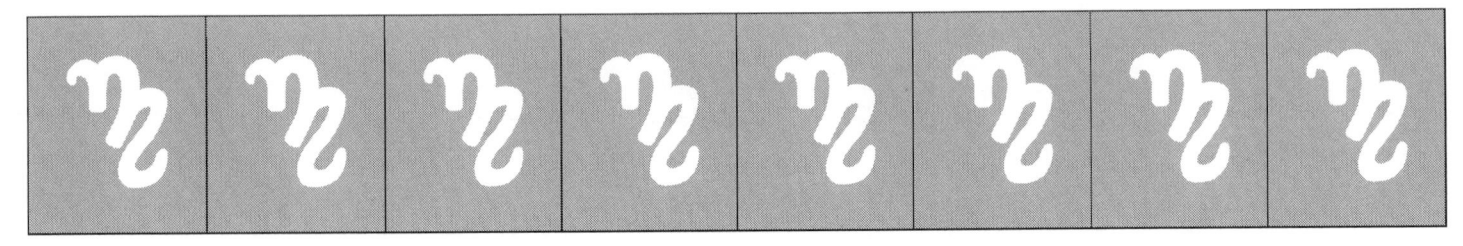

ㅁㄹㄹㄹㄹㄹㄹㄹ

T   T   T   T   T   T   T   T   T   T

T   T   T   T   T   T   T   T   T   T

T   T   T   T   T   T   T   T   T   T

T   T   T   T   T   T   T   T   T   T

T   T   T   T   T   T   T   T   T   T

T   T   T   T   T   T   T   T   T   T

T   T   T   T   T   T   T   T   T   T

T   T   T   T   T   T   T   T   T   T

T   T   T   T   T   T   T   T   T   T

M	D	B	F	M	G	I	L	M	A
P	J	S	U	H	Q	O	T	F	N
R	T	B	I	N	D	L	K	P	U
H	M	D	U	L	H	Q	N	F	I
C	T	U	B	R	E	G	M	D	L
N	G	S	K	L	M	J	C	M	R
R	Q	G	J	K	N	P	S	C	E

THEBAN SEARCH 13

BOTHER **BROTHER** **CLOSET** **FIGHTER** **QUARTER**
SUSPECT **TARGET** **TONGUE** **TSUNAMI** **TUNA**

ᚦᚦw ᚦᚦ Wᚦᚦᚦᚦ ᚦᚦᚦ ᚦᚦᚦᚦᚦᚦᚦᚦ

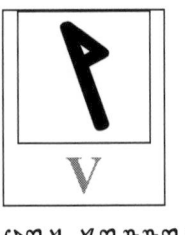

ᚤᚦᚦᚦᚦ

ᚦᚦᚦᚦᚦ ᚦᚦᚦᚦᚦ

ᚦᚦᚦᚦᚦᚦ - ᚦᚦᚦᚦᚦ

ᚦᚦᚦᚦᚦᚦᚦ

V	V	V	V	V	V	V	V	V	V

V	V	V	V	V	V	V	V	V	V

V	V	V	V	V	V	V	V	V	V

Traditional Corner

N   G   S   K   L   V   J   C   M   R

P   J   S   U   H   Q   O   T   F   N

R   T   B   V   N   D   L   K   P   U

C   T   U   B   R   E   G   M   D   L

H   M   V   U   L   H   Q   N   F   I

M   D   B   F   M   G   I   L   V   A

R   Q   G   J   K   N   P   S   C   E

THEBAN SEARCH 14

CHIVES
REVOLUTION

CRAVE
SAVE

HOVER
TELEVISION

MOVER
VIOLET

REVOLTING
VIOLIN

ᚦᚷᚲᚨ ᚷᚷ ᚦᚲᚾᚷᚲ ᚷᚷᚲ ᚲᚷᚷᚳᚲᚲᚷᚷ

ᚷᚷᚲᚷᚳᚲ - ᚷᚲᚷᚳᚲ

ᚲᚷᚲ ᚾᚳᚷᚲ ᚳᚷᚲᚲᚷᚷᚲ

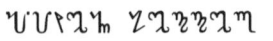

W

ᚢᚢᚲᚷᚲ ᚲᚷᚷᚷᚲᚷ

W W W W W W W W W W

W W W W W W W W W W

W W W W W W W W W W

Traditional Corner

_____ W _____ W _____ W _____ W _____ W _____ W _____ W _____ W _____ W _____ W

_____ W _____ W _____ W _____ W _____ W _____ W _____ W _____ W _____ W _____ W

_____ W _____ W _____ W _____ W _____ W _____ W _____ W _____ W _____ W _____ W

_____ W _____ W _____ W _____ W _____ W _____ W _____ W _____ W _____ W _____ W

_____ W _____ W _____ W _____ W _____ W _____ W _____ W _____ W _____ W _____ W

_____ W _____ W _____ W _____ W _____ W _____ W _____ W _____ W _____ W _____ W

C   D   B   F   W   G   I   L   V   A

P   J   S   U   H   Q   O   T   F   N

R   T   B   V   W   D   L   K   P   U

H   M   V   U   L   H   Q   N   F   I

C   W   U   B   R   E   G   M   D   W

N   G   S   K   L   V   J   C   M   R

R   Q   G   A   K   N   P   S   C   E

THEBAN SEARCH 15

BORROW
WATER

FLOWER
WINDOWS

MOWER
WORDSMITH

WALKING
WORLD

WALRUS
WRAPPER

ᚷᚾᚨ ᚨᚷ ᚨᚷᚢᚨᚷ ᚨᚷᚷ ᛘᚾᛋᚾᛚᚨᚷᚨ

X

ᚢᚢᚨᚷᚺ ᚷᚷᛋᚷᚷ

ᚨᚷᚷᚨᚷᚺ - ᚨᚷᚷᚷᚷ

Traditional Corner

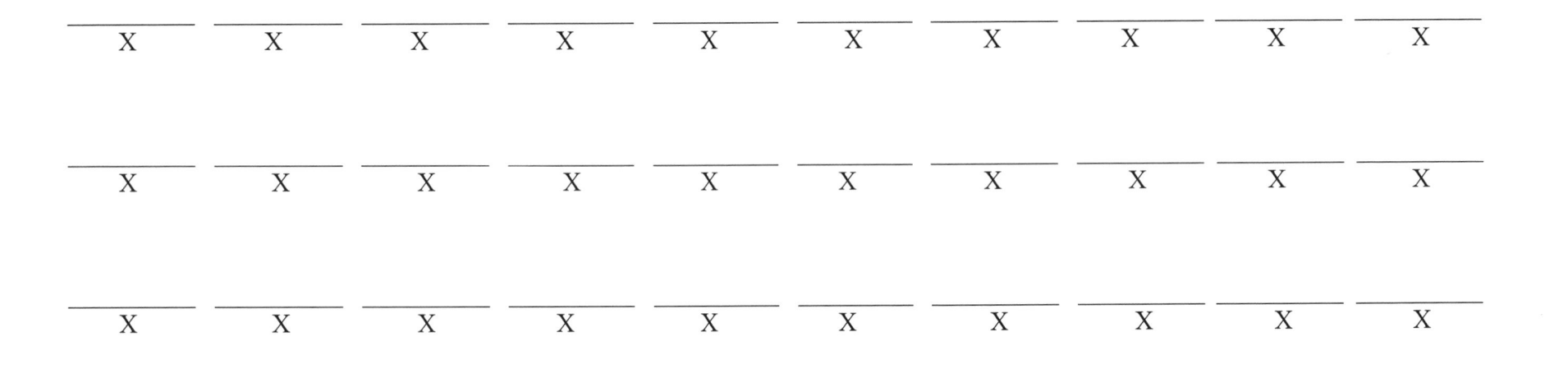

ᛘᚾᛚᛋᛋᚢᚾᚷ

X	X	X	X	X	X	X	X	X	X
X	X	X	X	X	X	X	X	X	X
X	X	X	X	X	X	X	X	X	X

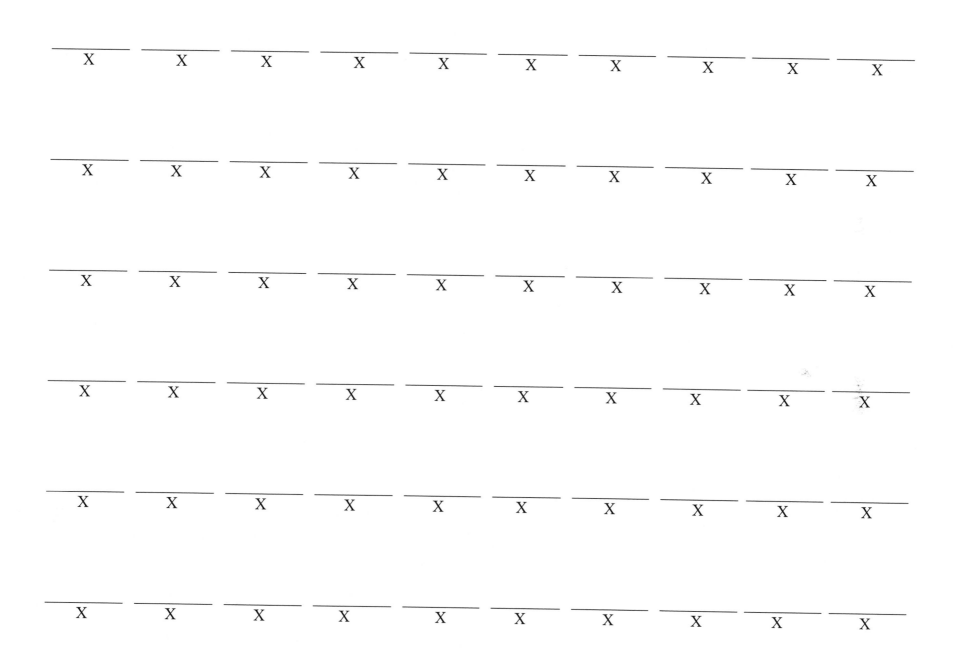

R	T	B	V	W	D	L	K	X	U
C	D	B	F	W	G	I	L	V	A
X	J	S	U	H	Q	O	T	F	N
N	G	S	K	L	V	J	C	M	R
H	M	V	U	L	H	Q	N	F	I
C	W	U	X	R	E	G	M	D	W
R	Q	G	A	K	N	P	S	C	E

THEBAN SEARCH 16

BEESWAX   **BOXERS**   **DIOXIN**   **DIXIELAND**   **EXTRA**

EXTREME   **FLAXEN**   **FOXTAIL**   **TOXINS**   **WAXING**

ꑞꑞꑞ ꑞꑞ ꑞꑞꑞꑞꑞ ꑞꑞꑞ ꑞꑞꑞꑞꑞꑞꑞ

Y

ꑞꑞꑞꑞꑞ ꑞꑞꑞꑞꑞꑞ

ꑞꑞꑞꑞꑞ - ꑞꑞꑞꑞ

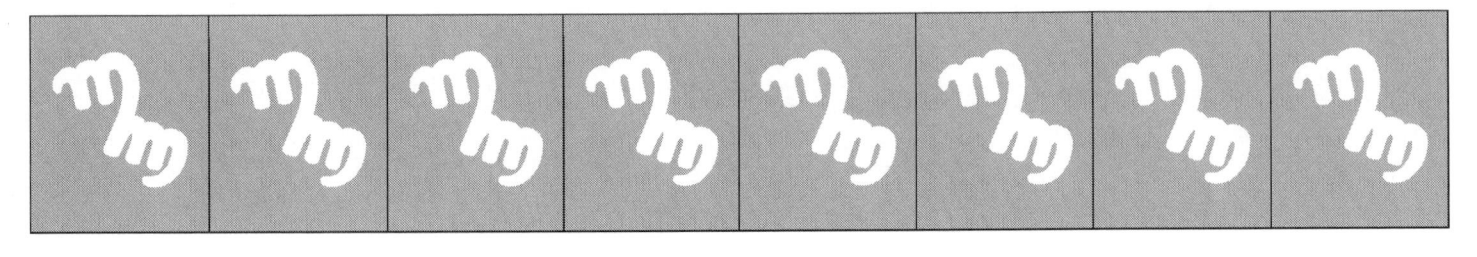

ꑞꑞꑞꑞꑞꑞꑞ

Y	Y	Y	Y	Y	Y	Y	Y	Y	Y

Y	Y	Y	Y	Y	Y	Y	Y	Y	Y

Y	Y	Y	Y	Y	Y	Y	Y	Y	Y

Traditional Corner

X   J   S   U   H   Q   O   T   F   N

R   T   B   V   W   D   L   K   X   U

R   Q   G   A   K   N   P   S   C   E

C   D   B   F   W   G   Y   L   V   A

H   M   V   U   L   Y   Q   N   F   I

N   G   S   K   Y   V   J   C   M   R

C   W   Y   X   R   E   G   M   D   W

THEBAN SEARCH 17

CRAYON WISKEY   **PAYOUT YELLOW**   **PLAYER YOGURT**   **RHYME YOKE**   **TRICYCLE YUMA**

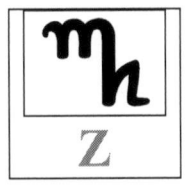

Z

ꤰꤰꤢ꤬ꤏ ꤢꤧꤒꤢ꤬ꤢꤩ

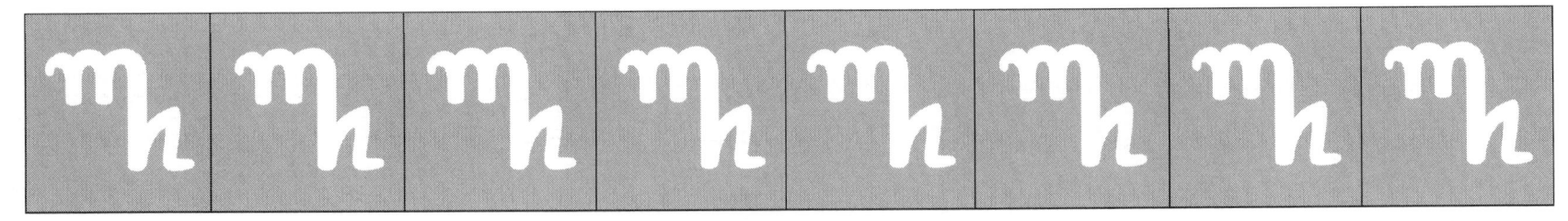

_____ Z _____ Z _____ Z _____ Z _____ Z _____ Z _____ Z _____ Z _____ Z _____ Z

_____ Z _____ Z _____ Z _____ Z _____ Z _____ Z _____ Z _____ Z _____ Z _____ Z

_____ Z _____ Z _____ Z _____ Z _____ Z _____ Z _____ Z _____ Z _____ Z _____ Z

Z Z Z Z Z Z Z Z Z Z

Z Z Z Z Z Z Z Z Z Z

Z Z Z Z Z Z Z Z Z Z

Z Z Z Z Z Z Z Z Z Z

Z Z Z Z Z Z Z Z Z Z

Z Z Z Z Z Z Z Z Z Z

H   M   V   U   Z   Y   Q   N   F   I

C   W   Y   X   R   E   G   M   D   W

N   G   S   K   Y   V   J   C   M   R

R   Q   G   A   K   N   P   Z   C   E

C   D   B   F   W   G   Y   L   V   A

X   J   S   U   H   Q   O   T   F   N

Z   T   B   V   W   D   L   K   X   U

THEBAN SEARCH 18

CZAR   **JACUZZI**   **JAZZED**   **MAZER**   **MAZURKA**
RAZOR   **SAZERAC**   **ZAMORA**   **ZEALOT**   **ZONURA**

ㅕㄲㅓ ㅋㄹ ㅄㅊㅄㅋㅏ ㅋㅓㅋ ㅋㅓㄱㄲㅓㄹㄱㅓㄺ

stop / .

ㅋㅄㅓㄺ ㄹㄱㅋㄹㄱㅓㄺ

ㄹㅋㄹㄱㅓㄺ - ㅋㄹㄺㅓㄹ

Traditional Corner

ㄲㄹㄱㄺㄹㅂㄱㅓㄺ

Z   T   B   V   W   D   L   K   X   U

H   M   V   U   Z   Y   Q   N   F   I

C   W   Y   X   R   E   G   M   D   W

N   G   S   K   Y   V   J   C   M   R

R   Q   G   A   .   N   P   Z   C   E

C   D   B   F   W   G   Y   L   V   .

X   J   .   U   H   Q   O   T   F   N

A	B	C	D	E	F	G	H	I	J	K	L	M	N	O	P	Q	R	S	T	U	V	W	X	Y	Z	.

SAMPLE PUZZLES

Decipher the Following Messages

(1)

(2)

A	B	C	D	E	F	G	H	I	J	K	L	M	N	O	P	Q	R	S	T	U	V	W	X	Y	Z	.

(3)

_____

(4)

_____

A	B	C	D	E	F	G	H	I	J	K	L	M	N	O	P	Q	R	S	T	U	V	W	X	Y	Z	.

(5)

Convert the Following Sentences into Theban

(1)

Running into the sunset will bring out the brightness in you.

_____

(2)

Drinking of the water will fill you.

_____

(3)

Birds fly, people walk, but do fish talk?

_____

(4)

Mountains are big, flowers are small, and streams are wide.

_____

Match the Following Words

Match up by drawing a line from the English word to the word in Theban

(1) DOG

(2) CAT

(3) FARM

(4) CHICKEN

(5) COW

(6) FARMER

(7) SWANS

(8) HAY

(9) FENCE

(10) BARN

(11) MILK

(12) EGGS

(13) CHEESE

(14) GOAT

(15) CORN

ㄱᄁ삶 (A)

ᄁᄔᄀᄀᄒᄀ (B)

ᄔᄀ諭 (C)

ᄁᄔᄂᄁᄃᄀᄂᄂ (D)

ᄔᄀᄒᄁᄀ (E)

ᄁᄁᄂ (F)

ᄁᄁᄁᄒ (G)

ᄔᄀᄁᄌᄀᄁ (H)

ᄒᄔᄀᄒᄒ (I)

ᄌᄂᄌᄃ (J)

ᄁᄀ삶 (K)

ᄃᄀᄁᄒ (L)

ᄔᄀᄁᄌ (M)

ᄁᄁᄒᄔ (N)

ᄂᄂᄂᄒ (O)

THEBAN SEARCH SOLUTIONS

THEBAN SEARCH 1

```
* D D * * * * * * E
* * E * * * * * E *
* * C A * * * F * *
* D A * D * F * * *
F A F * * A * * * *
A D E * C * * * F *
C * D E * * D A * *
E * D B E A D O O B
* * * * * E * * C *
* * * * * * * * * *
```

BEAD, BOO, COD, DAD, DEAD, DECAF, DEFACED, FACE, FADE, FEE

THEBAN SEARCH 2

```
B U G G E D * * * *
D * * * * * * * * *
* U * * * * * * * *
* * B B * D A * * D
* * E B E * D * * O
* E * G E * D * * O
F D G * * D E * * G
* A E * * E D U D *
B * * E * * * A * *
* * * * F * B F I G
```

ADDED, BAD, BAGGED, BEEF, BUGGED, DUBBED, DUDE, FEED, FIG, GOOD

THEBAN SEARCH 3

```
* * B E D * D * * C
* * * O I E * * * O
* * D H G G * * U
* G G G D I O D * G
E I U * E * E O U H
H H * H G U O D B F
* B A D G E H O G *
* * * O O * * * * *
* * * O D * * * * *
* * * G * * * * * *
```

BADGE, BOGIE, BOOGIE, COUGH, DODGE, DOGGED, DOUGH, FUDGE, GOOD, HIGH, HOG, HUGGED

THEBAN SEARCH 4

```
J * * G * * D * * *
O A U * * * J E * *
G O B * * * A * G *
D * * B * * C F * A
* * * * E * O A * *
E G D U J D B E * *
J * * A * * * D * *
* E D F I J I * * *
* E F * * * * * * *
D * * F * * * * * *
```

AGED, DEAF, DOUG, FIJI, JABBED, JACOB, JADED, JEFF, JOG, JUDGE

THEBAN SEARCH 5

```
B K * * * * * * K
E * C * * * * I C
D * * O * E * D O E
B A K E D K * K K *
K C E D * U E A * *
C J A C K D F * * *
* A O A * * * * * *
* * G K * * * * * *
* * * E E * * * * *
* * * * * * * * * *
```

BAKE, BED, CAGE, CAKE, COKE, DECK, DOCK, DUKE, FAKE, JACK, JOKE, KID

THEBAN SEARCH 6

```
H * L K * * * D * D
O * * L O * * U * O
L * H * A O * O * O
D * * A H B L L * F
* * * G I L F * * G
* * U D O L L O * O
* A * A K C O L O D
L * D * * * * * * G
* * * * * * * * * *
* * * * * * * * * *
```

DOGFOOD, DOLL, GOOFBALL, HAIL, HOLD, LAUGH, LOAD, LOCK, LOOK, LOUD

THEBAN SEARCH 7

```
*  *  *  *  *  *  *  L  *
*  *  *  *  *  *  D  A  *
B  E  E  F  C  A  K  E  E  *
C  *  M  D  *  M  *  B  M  *
*  A  L  I  O  *  *  A  *  *
*  O  B  D  L  *  D  C  *  *
G  *  E  B  *  K  *  L  *  *
*  L  K  L  A  H  C  E  O  *
*  *  *  *  *  G  *  *  *  M
H  O  M  E  *  *  E  *  *  *
```

BEEFCAKE, CABBAGE, CHALK, DEBACLE, GOLD, HOME, MEAL, MILK, MODEL, MOLD

THEBAN SEARCH 8

```
N  *  N  *  N  C  *  G  K  *
O  *  *  I  H  O  N  *  C  *
O  *  D  A  C  I  O  *  O  N
N  *  I  N  D  K  *  M  M  O
*  N  *  N  O  *  E  *  M  O
*  G  A  L  F  M  *  L  A  D
*  L  *  *  *  *  A  *  H  L
B  I  K  I  N  G  *  I  *  E
*  *  *  *  *  *  *  *  D  *
*  *  *  *  *  *  *  *  *  *
```

BIKING, CHAIN, DIAMOND, FLAG, HAMMOCK, LANDING, MOON, NICKEL, NOODLE, NOON

THEBAN SEARCH 9

```
N * * * N P * G * J
E * * A L * N * * A
K * L U N I * * * P
C P M * P A * * * A
I P * M H A P P E N
H * U K * * * K * *
C J * N * P * * I *
* * * I * * M * * N
* * * P * * * U * *
D N U O P * * * D *
```

CHICKEN, DUMP, HAPPEN, JAPAN, JUMPING, NAPKIN, PINK, PLAN, PLUMP, POUND

THEBAN SEARCH 10

```
K C I U Q * * * * *
E U Q A L C * E Q *
* * * * I E * U * *
Q * * N U * E Q * *
E U Q Q * E Q N * *
* U A * N * U A * *
E L Q C * * A M * *
P * * I K * R * * *
* * * * L * K * * *
* Q U I N C E * * *
```

CINQUE, CLAQUE, CLIQUE, MANQUE, PLAQUE, QUACK, QUARK, QUEEN, QUICK, QUINCE

THEBAN SEARCH 11

```
* * * * * R * F * *
E * * * O * A * * *
R * * B * R * * * R
U E I * M * R * * A
G N G L E U Q E R P
I R A N O * * * * I
F N A F A * * * * D
D * G E O R G E * *
* * * * B * * * * *
* * * E C A R * * *
```

BEAR, FARMLAND, FIGURE, FOUR, GEORGE, PREQUEL, RACE, RANGER, RAPID, ROBIN

THEBAN SEARCH 12

```
S * S A R D I N E S
H H M C * * * * A *
O C A * A * * M * S
P R E C * L U * S *
P A B * L R L E * *
I E N * A A N O * *
N S O I * I S * P *
G * O * S * * S * S
* * M U S U C R I C
* * B S I N G E R *
```

BUSINESS, CIRCUS, CLASS, MOONBEAMS, SAMURAI, SARDINES, SCALLOPS, SEARCH, SHOPPING, SINGER

THEBAN SEARCH 13

```
E T I * T * * R * B
U A * M * E E * O *
G R R * A H S T * *
N G E S T N H O * *
O E T O U E U A L *
T T R * R S N S * C
* B A * * U P * T *
* * U * T * * E * *
* * Q * * * * * C *
F I G H T E R * * T
```

BOTHER, BROTHER, CLOSET, FIGHTER, QUARTER, SUSPECT, TARGET, TONGUE, TSUNAMI, TUNA

THEBAN SEARCH 14

```
R E V O L T I N G R
* E * E * * V O * E
* * V * C I * I * V
* A * O O H V S * O
S * * L H * I I * M
N O I T U L O V E R
* N * * * * L E E *
E V A R C * E L * S
* * * * * * T E * *
* * * * * * * T * *
```

CHIVES, CRAVE, HOVER, MOVER, REVOLTING, REVOLUTION, SAVE, TELEVISION, VIOLET, VIOLIN

THEBAN SEARCH 15

```
* W * W W * W * W *
R * O A O I * S R *
* E T R N R U * A W
* E W D D R L * P O
R * O O L S * D P R
* W * A L * M * E R
S * W * * F * I R O
G N I K L A W * T B
M O W E R * * * * H
* * * * * * * * * *
```

BORROW, FLOWER, MOWER, WALKING, WALRUS, WATER, WINDOWS, WORDSMITH, WORLD, WRAPPER

THEBAN SEARCH 16

```
N F * N * * S * D B
I * O * E N * N * E
X * * X I X A * * E
O * * X T L A * * S
I * O * E A B L * W
D T * I * O I * F A
* * X * X * * L * X
* I * E X T R E M E
D * R G N I X A W *
* S * * E X T R A *
```

BEESWAX, BOXERS, DIOXIN, DIXIELAND, EXTRA, EXTREME, FLAXEN, FOXTAIL, TOXINS, WAXING

THEBAN SEARCH 17

```
* * * * * * * * R Y
C R A Y O N * * E O
E L C Y C I R T Y G
T * E * E H * E A U
* U * K Y L K * L R
* * O M O S L * P T
* * E Y I Y * O * *
* * * W A M U Y W *
* * * * * P * * * *
* * * * * * * * * *
```

CRAYON, PAYOUT, PLAYER, RHYME, TRICYCLE, WISKEY, YELLOW, YOGURT, YOKE, YUMA

THEBAN SEARCH 18

```
* * D * * * * Z A *
* M * E * * A R R *
C A * * Z M O * U *
* Z * J O Z * * N *
* U A R A * A * O *
* R A R * C * J Z *
* K * * * * U * * *
S A Z E R A C Z * *
T O L A E Z * * Z *
* M A Z E R * * * I
```

CZAR, JACUZZI, JAZZED, MAZER, MAZURKA, RAZOR, SAZERAC, ZAMORA, ZEALOT, ZONURA

SAMPLE PUZZLE SOLUTIONS

(1) Don't cry because it's over. Smile because it happened. (Dr. Suess)
(2) Shoot for the moon. Even if you miss, you'll land among the stars. (Norman Vincent Peale)
(3) Think for yourself and let others enjoy the privilege of doing so too. (Voltaire)
(4) The most wasted of all days is one without laughter. (E. E. Cummings)
(5) It is good to have an end to journey toward; but it is the journey that matters, in the end. (Ernest Hemmingway)

Convert the Following Sentences into Theban

(1)

ꟿꟾꜱꜱꜲꜱꜲꟿ Ꜳꜱꟿꟿ ꟾꟾꟿ ꟿ...

(2)

ꟿꟾꜲꜱꜱꜲ...

(3)

...?

(4)

...

Match the Following Words

1=F

2=K

3=M

4=D

5=N

6=H

7=I

8=C

9=E

10=L

11=J

12=O

13=B

14=A

15=G

A	B	C	D	E	F	G
૫	૧	૫	૧	૧	૫	૫

H	I	J	K	L	M	N
૫	૫	૫	૫	૫	૫	૫

O	P	Q	R	S	T	U
૫	૫	૫	૫	૪	૫	૫

V	W	X	Y	Z	END / .	*Word Separator
૫	૫	૫	૫	૫	૫	•

MASTER THEBAN TABLE

* The "•" is sometimes used to separate words and is optional.
For example: ૫૧૫૫૫•૫૫૫૫૫૫ ૫૫•૫૫૫૫•૫૫૫૫૫